# Gruff Colouring

## Adult Colouring for Burly Men

by J. Benson

ISBN-10: 1519780656
ISBN-13: 978-1519780652

The *Gruff Colouring* book is crammed with mindful colouring, perfect for burly men who need some down time.

Full of rocking designs that are relaxing and a pleasure to colour, the resulting patterns are full tilt awesome to the max.

Sure, your mates would ridicule you if they found out what you're doing, so why not tear out each page and burn/blend/eat* it after colouring to hide your secret - it's the journey, not the destination that counts.

*Dispose of spent pages responsibly. The author shall not be held responsible for injury caused by fire or ink poisoning and/or damage to kitchen appliances.

# Gruff Colouring

## Adult Colouring for Burly Men

# Gruff Colouring

## Adult Colouring for Burly Men

# Gruff Colouring

## Adult Colouring for Burly Men

# Gruff Colouring

## Adult Colouring for Burly Men

# Gruff Colouring

## Adult Colouring for Burly Men

# Gruff Colouring

## Adult Colouring for Burly Men

# Gruff Colouring

## Adult Colouring for Burly Men

# Gruff Colouring

## Adult Colouring for Burly Men

# Gruff Colouring

## Adult Colouring for Burly Men

# Gruff Colouring

## Adult Colouring for Burly Men

# Gruff Colouring

## Adult Colouring for Burly Men

# Gruff Colouring

## Adult Colouring for Burly Men

# Gruff Colouring

## Adult Colouring for Burly Men

# Gruff Colouring

## Adult Colouring for Burly Men

# Gruff Colouring

## Adult Colouring for Burly Men

# Interlude

# You have a voice

Are you enjoying your experience? The world wants to hear your voice! Whether you love or loath this book, your feedback can make all the difference when someone is deciding whether it's right for them! When you have the opportunity, please visit Amazon or your favorite social network and share your thoughts by leaving a review or rating of this book.

Thank you,


Jack

# Gruff Colouring

## Adult Colouring for Burly Men

# Gruff Colouring

## Adult Colouring for Burly Men

# Gruff Colouring

## Adult Colouring for Burly Men

# Gruff Colouring

## Adult Colouring for Burly Men

# Gruff Colouring

Adult Colouring for Burly Men

# Gruff Colouring

## Adult Colouring for Burly Men

# Gruff Colouring

## Adult Colouring for Burly Men

# Gruff Colouring

## Adult Colouring for Burly Men

# Gruff Colouring

## Adult Colouring for Burly Men

# Gruff Colouring

Adult Colouring for Burly Men

# Gruff Colouring

## Adult Colouring for Burly Men

# Gruff Colouring

## Adult Colouring for Burly Men

# Gruff Colouring

## Adult Colouring for Burly Men

# Gruff Colouring

## Adult Colouring for Burly Men

# Gruff Colouring

## Adult Colouring for Burly Men

# Gruff Colouring

## Adult Colouring for Burly Men

# Gruff Colouring

## Adult Colouring for Burly Men

# Gruff Colouring

## Adult Colouring for Burly Men

# Gruff Colouring

## Adult Colouring for Burly Men

# Gruff Colouring

## Adult Colouring for Burly Men

# Gruff Colouring

## Adult Colouring for Burly Men

# Gruff Colouring

## Adult Colouring for Burly Men

# Gruff Colouring

## Adult Colouring for Burly Men

# Gruff Colouring

## Adult Colouring for Burly Men

# Gruff Colouring

## Adult Colouring for Burly Men

# Gruff Colouring

## Adult Colouring for Burly Men

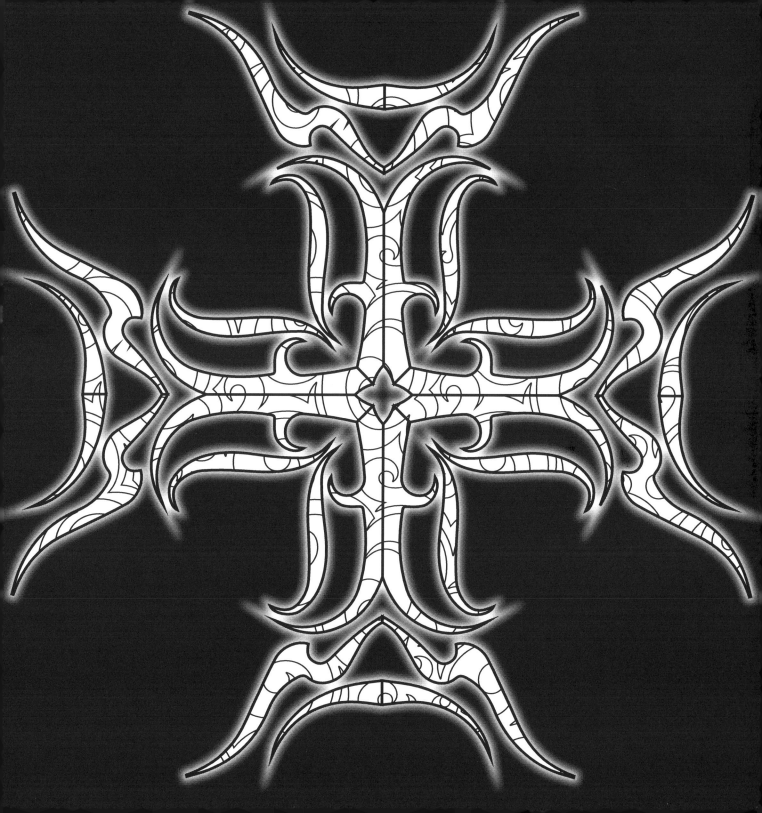

# Gruff Colouring

## Adult Colouring for Burly Men

# Gruff Colouring

## Adult Colouring for Burly Men

# Gruff Colouring

## Adult Colouring for Burly Men

# Gruff Colouring

## Adult Colouring for Burly Men

# Gruff Colouring

## Adult Colouring for Burly Men

# Gruff Colouring

## Adult Colouring for Burly Men

# Gruff Colouring

## Adult Colouring for Burly Men

# Gruff Colouring

## Adult Colouring for Burly Men

Now that you've completed this book, why not cut out your favorite patterns and share them with the people you care about...

48373982R00064

Made in the USA
Lexington, KY
28 December 2015